SPUN OUT

SPUN OUT

Five Crucial Steps to Restored Hope and Healthy Endurance

Troy D. Larsen

ELM HILL

A Division of
HarperCollins Christian Publishing

www.elmhillbooks.com

Spun Out
Five Crucial Steps to Restored Hope and Healthy Endurance

Published in Nashville, Tennessee, by Elm Hill, an imprint of Thomas Nelson. Elm Hill and Thomas Nelson are registered trademarks of HarperCollins Christian Publishing, Inc.

Elm Hill titles may be purchased in bulk for educational, business, fund-raising, or sales promotional use. For information, please e-mail SpecialMarkets@ ThomasNelson.com.

Library of Congress Cataloging-in-Publication Data

Library of Congress Control Number: 2018960785

ISBN 978-1-400303113 (Paperback)
ISBN 978-1-400303595 (Hardbound)
ISBN 978-1-400303618 (eBook)

For my friends and friends to be made,
who share their stories, and together hope and
encouragement are found.

CONTENTS

PROLOGUE

There are various reasons for waking up each morning and making the decision to carry on. Life has a way of creating certain demands that make us motivated and moved to step out the day ahead. It never ceases to amaze me how many individuals on the outward appearance have it together and are living out what appears to be their perfect protected life, yet after spending any amount of time with them, truth revealing there are many challenges present that will surface. We identify with one of two categories: first, life is great and we believe we are immune to overload and being overextended. Second, the reality of these could not be more apparent, complete and total understanding exist. In reality, struggles are very real and challenges of life have either taken a serious toll or fear lies in what may come or may not come. We have a way of presenting ourselves as whole, complete, and fully satisfied. We have trained ourselves to not fully acknowledge our real condition as we may appear weak or vulnerable.

The events of July 1, 2016, began a perspective that changed the way I viewed life, exposing a process that sparked this writing. What started as a perfect evening ended in a series of events and dialog that brought about the teaching and message of this book. Moments of living life lead us into discoveries we would never think of while alone with our thought process.

Encouragement can seem quite distant in times of being overextended, less than appreciated, and misunderstood. Our Life that once held dreams, stop, planned events do not take place, loved ones are lost, ideas become stuck, and goals seem out of reach. This place that I call "Spun Out," a short period of time or one that lasts for extended seasons, does not seem to resolve or go away. The reality of knowing life is at a full mark, a wall, a question of how hard to keep driving forward becomes a constant reminder of a condition we did not expect or plan for. There are answers, proven methods and solid foundations to build upon to find encouragement when Spun Out. With these five crucial steps, my encouragement to you is that you will find restored hope and walk in healthy endurance.

Troy

STEP ONE

REST

CHAPTER 1

WHEN THE PROPELLER STOPS

"We should always believe the best, never expect the worst, and trust that our life is truly being guided through the intricate details of each daily experience."

Troy

Magic Reservoir is our family's favorite water ski lake in Central Idaho. Winter gives way to spring, and the reservoirs of the west fill with a full brim of fresh water. As summer carries on, water levels subside due to necessary irrigation demands and many new hidden rock gardens, along with the appearance of logs and sandbars arise. When the water is low we take note of where not to drive the boat, as the water creeps lower later in the summer. We plan seriously the clear open stretches in our water pathways for long, straight water ski pulls.

This reservoir fills a number of offshoot canyons that have towering walls of ancient volcanic rock walls. The waterways meander around and leave spectacular sights to see, a perfect block from the wind creating still, glassy water that is pure water skiers' delight. Because of these natural wonders, visiting Magic is a regular stop for us all summer long.

July 1, 2016 was a night of delightful warmth, flat smooth water, and a lake completely full to the highest water mark. We had had an extraordinary winter runoff, which left the reservoir full to capacity. We could not have been more thrilled having this first chance of skiing for the year. Our family—my wife Linda, daughter Julia, son Curtis, and our friend Dakota—spent the first part of the evening exploring the lake's Camas Creek lava canyon. We decided to start our water ski and wakeboard sets in the narrow, still, quiet, and secluded waters. Julia was up first. She slipped into the cool water off the swim deck of our Centurion ski boat. The rope tightened and with a nod of approval, our evening of pulling began—back and forth on the water behind a ski boat at its best!

Then, with a hand raised and a voice of protest, Julia came to a stop in the middle of the lake. There is only one reason you sink when holding a towrope behind a ski boat—the boat stops! We were in the center of the water channel when from seemingly out of nowhere, the boat hit something hard, solid, and had no give. Immediately all that seemed so right went drastically wrong. We had forgotten that in this lava canyon there was a column of rocks that stand up in the middle of the waterway. With the water high, the rocks were hidden 16 inches under the surface, the perfect depth to destroy a direct driveline, rudder, and propeller of a ski boat. It was from this experience that I would see clearly a parallel to our life that would change our broken heart, discouraged soul, and depleted physical endurance. It was here that truths were uncovered, perspectives changed, and encouragement would begin. Crucial steps came about as a result of our boat hitting the rock, the evening opening up my understanding of the rocks closely beneath the surface of my own life and others' as well.

The propeller stopped immediately. Steering ceased as the rudder was gone. It seemed time stopped while we were in a quandary about what happened. We quickly went from moving forward to sitting still. From everything being so right to being so wrong. Plans changed, all motion went to survival mode as we thought we had punched a hole in the hull that would sink the boat. Living life will bring moments that seem to bring us to a grinding halt or at least a momentary stop. Everyone has their story, their life to walk out, their moments of being totally still.

That still moment is that gap in time when we desperately try to wrap our thought process around what has happened. This can be a short moment or, in some cases, a lengthy span of time when we feel utterly lost to what is happening. Human experiences may vary by their nature, yet they remain essentially similar to those whose story we do not know.

The night we hit the hidden rock, the propeller was a complete taco, severely bent and folded over edges that allowed for close to zero propulsion to get back to the boat landing. We had lost our rudder that was broken off at the stern of the boat. The only way to steer and set direction was to use our emergency paddle as a rudder. The drive shaft that turns the propeller was bent sharply, shaking the boat profusely as it tried to drive forward.

In our lives, we can identify with what we call "events." We are presented moments that are difficult to ignore, things that happen we wish had not. It is here where honesty sets in: we could be, and have been, hit—we are not immune to a condition in life I call Spun Out.

No one is immune to the circumstances of life, but what we do during these times makes all the difference to our long-term well-being. Most concerning are those who believe they are somehow exempt from the rocks of life. It is wise to do everything in our ability to plan, organize, and prepare for a smooth sail through life, but even with the best intentions, we still live in a world where those silly rocks exist. It is not that we focus on the dangers and harmful possibilities and become frozen in fear, but rather that we walk wisely, avoiding unnecessary hits and stops. Some personal questions to ask are:

Where do I find encouragement in difficult times?
When discouraged, how do I obtain hope?
What is my source for personal endurance?

It is important from a broad point of view to see that the propellers in our lives—those things that drive and move us forward—can and will over time become worn, need attention, require rest, and at times may become broken and need full repair.

Unexpected groundings—we will all experience them. We do not necessarily plan for the unexpected abrupt stops in our life. It can be easy, as individuals with strong personal drive and faith in that which we have set out to accomplish to embrace the idea of being exempt from interruptions in our life. It is common to ignore possible setbacks and treat them as insignificant, as if they will not happen to us or slow us down. We tend to observe others in their life events and decide that their struggles are rooted in the way they choose to live. It is easy to pass judgment on others when we are experiencing smooth sailing; it is easy to observe and hold an opinion of others until we personally experience a knock ourselves. We should always believe the best, never expect the worst, and trust that our life is truly being guided through the intricate detail of each daily experience.

> *Who shall separate us from the love of Christ? Shall trouble, hardship, persecution, famine, nakedness, danger, or sword? As it is written: "For your sake we face death all day long; we are considered as sheep to be slaughtered."*
>
> *No, in all these things we are more than conquerors through him who loved us.*
>
> (NIV: ROMANS 8: 35–37)

CHAPTER 2

SPEAKING OF SHIPS

"One brings despair and death to the soul, the other brings hope and life."

Troy

Shipwrecks present a reality of complete loss. No matter the cause, past or present, ship disasters entail great losses with respect to the vessel, cargoes, passengers, and crew. Ships that found their way to the bottom of the ocean become legends and lost to most of the known world, reserved only for explorers of the sea or tales from the few who managed to survive. Ships are majestic and carry a glory that few other objects can claim. Ships have provided transportation to both the known and unknown remote parts of the world. Precious goods traveled the high seas for years, with new adventures upon each voyage. Ships have great purpose. There is truly a magic and mystery to ships.

I truly believed for a time—after many years of high output, unrealistic expectations, and fast pace—that my life had come to rest in a state of shipwreck. It was in the illusive concept of my life a shipwrecked state that being overdriven, overextended, underappreciated, in despair, and hitting a stopping point made this seem like a reality. The thought of a shipwrecked life sent red flags and warning signs of not staying the course with my life. There was no room to back off the pace of life for a season. I could not slow down, and those around me in leadership could not see or understand the need to pull back the pace. It is never convenient for an organization with a strong emphasis on growth to allow those around them to back off, as it does not seemingly promote growth. The problem with this mindset is that the right direction to correctly evaluate our true condition is rarely made known until we are burned out. The feeling of never doing enough and not being important like the individuals doing what appears to be outstanding and worthy of praise can begin to haunt our mind. It is human nature to underestimate who we are and what we do as being valuable and meaningful. We must adjust our thinking and realize that in reality, the things we have accomplished personally are unique and have great worth.

There is a place of a true shipwrecked life: when one runs oneself into the ground and repeatedly denies help from others. There is a point where turning away from faith and principles that guide our life can bring about personal destruction. Harm, pain, despair, and misery may be present, yet the truth is as long as one is willing to change and find rescue, there is always a way of escape and options to be found. If you consider yourself shattered, broken, lost, and damaged at the core of your being, there is a means to being renewed and expectant of recovery and hope.

Repairs to the Centurion ski boat after our shattering grounding event brought us to an incredible life-changing discovery. Here is that story.

We delivered our boat by trailer to a professional boat repair shop in Boise, Idaho. I placed a rebuilt propeller in the stern of the boat to be provided to the service technician as a replacement to the cracked, bent, and folded propeller that remained after our incident. Upon inspection with the technician, we looked at and evaluated all that would be necessary to repair and restore all broken parts to their correct operating condition. After notes were taken and parts evaluated, I pointed out the rebuilt propeller to be used in place of buying a new propeller, reasoning that it should be sufficient. It was at this moment when words spoken brought light and introspection to the shipwrecked life illusion.

"You know," with a voice of insight and concern the technician spoke, "I recently watched a documentary on ships. Ships are large and must be fine-tuned. Few people take the time to understand the importance of what is happening under the hull of a ship when it is in motion. If the propeller is not perfectly in balance, the vessel will shake and cause further damage due to vibration, causing extreme wear over time. When a propeller has been damaged or worn over time, which is what commonly happens, it will send a ship out of service. It is at this point a ship will undergo dry dock. Dry docking a ship allows propellers that weigh thousands of pounds to be reformed and completely remolded even multiple times. This process can at times take several years. During this time, all repairs and restorations that need to be made to the ship are attended to as the vessel rests in an accessible position out of the water. Not only the exterior of the ship undergoes repair and restoration, but the interior of the ship can also be completely changed and made new. It is with this in mind that I recommend starting over with a new, fully balanced propeller."

The shipwreck mentality instantly called into contrast the dry-dock mentality, as if a bright light was turned on to shed understanding on the difference between the two scenarios. One brings despair and death to the soul, the other brings hope and life. This brought an outstanding opportunity to my life view, as what might have been seen as lost, forgotten, sunk, grounded, placed on hold, crushed, and broken took on a new direction of renewed expectation. For all of us, what appears, or may appear as lost, will take new shape and structure and move forward finding fresh rejuvenated life. The good news is, we are not shipwrecked: we are simply in *dry dock* for a season!

From the end of the earth I will cry to You, when my heart is overwhelmed; Lead me to the rock that is higher than I.

(NKJV: PSALM 61:2)

CHAPTER 3

DRY DOCK

"*Dry dock* is both planned and unplanned. Both are the same place but represent drastically different circumstances."

Troy

It is mostly unheard of for individuals to speak of planned time for rest and restoration. We are quite driven to keep pushing and pursuing our plans and goals without letting up. We are encouraged to do this by social pressure and structure, the unspoken "more is better" to a better life; after all, we need to live life to the full. In this information age, there are ever-increasing suggestions and pressures to every facet of our lives. "More is better" is presented in possessions, business, education, home, recreation activities, church, and even vacations. Vacations are the closest we come to planned rest. In many circumstances we come home more exhausted than when we left, somehow we miss the rest and restoration part. There is a healthy place for our life I call *dry dock*, a state of necessary rest.

A dry dock is a narrow basin that can be flooded to allow a ship to be floated in, then drained to allow that ship to come to rest on a dry platform.

Dry dock is both planned and unplanned. Both are the same place but represent drastically different circumstances. Most often *dry dock* is not where we expect to come to a place of rest, stopped. Planned dry dock from a working ship's perspective comes from a knowledge of how much travel and use can be made before repairs and maintenance are necessary. Many factors play into each ship's needs, including environment, intended use, and function. A good example of this are the massive ships that dredge the Columbia River at the mouth of the Pacific Ocean. The U.S. Army Corps of Engineers, Portland Oregon District, operate the ships *Essayons* and *Yaquina* to keep the channels clear for a variety of other ships coming into port. These large work ships are dry-docked annually for repair and restoration to keep them in top operating condition. Due to the need of keeping the channel depth sufficient and free of collecting sediment, these ships cannot afford to be out of service due to unattended and preventable mechanical failure. *Essayons* and *Yaquina* have a mandatory dry dock period. It is worthy to note that many ships have arranged dry docks scheduled specifically to keep them in excellent working condition.

Then there are those ships that end up in dry dock for a variety of reasons, unforeseen damage that occurs, in most instances at inopportune timing. Storms, groundings, mechanical failures, personnel mistakes, collisions with other vessels, and precarious situations all cause unforeseen damage. This can be explained with the phrase, "Let's just say … something happened." Dry-docking deals with what is unseen, the bottom of the vessel, the haul, the driveline, the rudder, and the propeller. All of these are of utmost importance, as the ship simply does not receive power for movement, steering, or floating without these vital components. Consider this: Approximately 40 percent of a loaded ship is below the waterline. Both in ships and in our lives, there is a substantial amount of events taking place in the unseen portion of our life story.

When a ship or our life is in *dry dock*, it is virtually out of commission and not doing what it is intended to do—sail. On the other hand, a ship in dry dock is much better off than a ship that is wrecked, as the ship in repair will sail again. The shipwrecked life is lost in history as a tragedy with many hanging questions, many unknowns, and begging for answers of how this tragedy could have been prevented.

Dry dock pertaining to our life is about getting the necessary rest, repair, care, and restoration so that we can be useful again.

When a ship is in dry dock, small or large amounts of time may be needed to complete the repair. It is easy to place scheduled timelines on our seasons of *dry dock*, as we tend to underestimate our accurate condition. As with ships and our lives, these predetermined timelines typically take longer than our initial evaluation due to the complexity of the underlying details. It is of utmost importance to embrace the process and allow room for full completion in the *dry- dock* process. Repairs in the unseen underwater portions reveal hidden damages, and with exposure comes reality and truth. When we see our condition in the open, the realization of our true state becomes clear. We tend to focus on the visible, above-waterline areas of our life, since they are always glaring at us and pointed out more readily by those around us. In many instances, the interior of a ship will take on a makeover and the surface of the exterior is sanded and refinished while in dry dock. Our lives parallel these processes when we allow a season of *dry dock*. Stopping at the appropriate time before excessive wear and tear sets in is always best, as this allows us to avoid long-term damage. Then there are those cases wherein we find ourselves in a *dry dock* state not necessarily by choice but when we are forced there due to not stopping at the appropriate time until damage has been done. We should realize that this is a place of God-given rest. It is unfortunate that *dry dock* is not readily spoken of as a normal asset of our life, but rather the glory of the ship at full throttle ahead. Much is spoken about where we are going, what we are doing, and how quickly we are going to get there without the plan and organization of how this will be completed and accomplished. We must realize that there is no shame in taking a given time to become healthy, rested, and ready to reengage with operating at full-speed ahead.

For those who face these questions: Can I and Do I have the strength to go on? Do I have what it takes to regroup, pick up, and move on again?

You find yourself identifying with the shipwreck lodged upon the rocks of life. Dreams have been broken, plans altered and changed, what once was full of life now appears to be lost and in some cases that which was life is gone; hope is faint, victory and vitality appear lost. The answer to these questions is yes, there is a *dry dock* waiting for you where there is a new reality for you to be pulled off the rocks and brought to healthy endurance and restored hope.

There is a hope that goes beyond every natural hope. Not a fairy tale, wishing-well hope. Not a hope devised by how positive we can think. Not a hope in great people, peaceful places, or manufactured things. The best definition of hope working in its true and purest function is as I heard spoken by Graham Cook, "Divine Expectation." Understanding the depth, strength, and power of hope through the eyes of Divine Expectation will transform your perspective. It is through events written in scripture that we acquire encouragement, that encouragement leads to endurance that in turn produces hope. It is by being taught the right information about God, who He is and what He desires for us that hope is built. God's Words are the greatest encouragement I know. His workings and dealing with humanity are revealed throughout scripture, and He truly is the lifter of the discouraged. His nature has been given expression through the life and actions of His Son Jesus Christ who was the exact representation and picture of who God is. God is the God of concrete expectation. Hope with the right expectation in the correct context will change the way we view the final outcome of our circumstances and situations drastically.

The definition of Divine is: relating to or proceeding directly from God.

The definition of Expectation is: the act or state of expecting; anticipation, assurance.

Divine expectation is placing our anticipation and assurance in the living God, in the power of Jesus Christ and all that has been provided and purchased for us through Him.

Divine expectation goes beyond what our natural mind can process on its own. An expectation that is deep rooted in knowing Jesus and hope that is provided for us through Him. Assurance in God is a hope beyond our natural reasoning that runs deeper than what the heart and mind can imagine. Expectation in God takes the wall, the bog, the grounding, the pain, the diagnosed, the broken, the hurting, the outcast, the fallen, the burned out, the whatever you are that is on the *dry dock* and breathes life into it. This is true hope, a divine expectation that you are not a ship-wreck but rather ready to rest, be remolded, and cared for, brought back to one day set out and sail again. Times of *dry dock* are seasons all their own. They are a process, and embracing the hope and encouragement they provide are not only necessary but incredibly healthy.

May the God of hope fill you with all joy and peace as you trust in him, so that you may overflow with hope by the power of the Holy Spirit.

(ROMANS 15: 13)

Why are you downcast, O my soul? Why so disturbed within me? Put your hope in God, for I will yet praise him, my Savior and my God.

(PSALM 42:11–12)

STEP TWO

EVALUATION

CHAPTER 4

SEASONS

"There is a time to rest and a time to work with great determination."

Troy

Seasons, we all have our favorite. For my family and me, winter has been a favorite season. There is something magical about snow-covered fields with ice crystals glimmering like thousands of diamonds in the silver light of a full moon. A team of sled dogs pulling in harness, panting steamy breath in the freezing cold air with pitter-pattering on the snow beneath their feet, the sled runners gliding smoothly close behind over the snow. Going for walks with loved ones in soft fluffy white powder and snowflakes falling from the sky quieting and softening the world around. Pointing ski tips downhill from the top of a steep mountain to swoosh back and forth with the speed and freedom of a flying bird. Crisp air when touching the skin or breathed in awakens the senses with distinction and clarity that this is winter, this is cold. Repetitively I spoke the words, "Five degrees Fahrenheit is my favorite temperature," for it is here that the sled runners slide fast, dogs and mushers don't overheat, and winter is at its best, not too cold and not too warm. It is because of this our family named our sled dog kennel Five Degrees. I could really go on and on about winter—it is endearing and holds a special place in our heart. Then again, summer....

Natural seasons are divided into winter, spring, summer, and fall, which all in their own right have distinction and value. So it is with *dry docks*: they have distinction and value. They are a process and each portion is important. It is easy to get uneasy and want to prioritize one aspect of *dry dock* when in reality we need to embrace the entire process or seasons they contain. I am highlighting natural seasons, as when we see the necessity and value of each, we also see and appreciate the seasons in our life. We understand for the most part what each natural season holds in terms of temperature and weather, dependent upon geographical location and climate. Living in the mountains of Idaho allows a crisp distinction between each season. Winter: cold temperatures and blankets of white snow; spring: warming temperatures, thawing ice, bright wildflowers; summer: green leaves, ample sunshine, and warmth; fall: cooling temperatures, with foliage in bright colors.

In terms of orchards and fruit-bearing trees, harvest (the finished product) is typically thought of as the pinnacle of the seasons. It is the reward, the final goal of all the planning, nurturing, and preparation that has been invested to get finally to harvest. It is all too easy to miss and forget what is required to get to the final harvest. There is a great danger in making the assumption that harvest is the end-all. We must not neglect each and every other season that is required to arrive at final harvest, for each season is required to remain healthy. If we look at harvest as the ideal place of fulfillment and do not place value on the other seasons, we will miss contentment and never be satisfied. Without fully understanding the magnitude of the labor associated with harvest, we tend to overemphasize the importance of visibly working and doing. Harvest is incredible effort and hard work. It is impossible both in a natural and figurative sense to always be engaged in harvest. It is here that the value of each season is not only seen as necessary but greatly appreciated.

Seasons have purpose! If we glorify and exalt one season over another and forget or discard the purposes all the other seasons have, we will become skewed in our view and become out of balance. It does not matter how much I appreciate the season of winter; the other seasons provide enjoyment and are necessary. As much as I like cold, I sure would not want to live in it all the time. There have been times when gripped in winter's cold, I could not want anything more than for the season to change to summer, fast. Likewise, if our emphasis becomes heavily weighted in one passion or direction, we will come to conclusions of our worldview and those around us that are incorrect and judgmental. When we place value upon different seasons, it is much easier to respect others in their segment of life. It is here that we must take a deeper look at what we value and focus on it. It may require looking back and recognizing what we have done and what motivated us, asking questions of ourselves as to why we have been doing what we have been doing. Also, looking forward with anticipation for what can be done recognizing the season we have been in. So many individuals feel as if they were doing nothing important when in all reality they are comparing themselves to the wrong season and are in exactly the correct place. When we understand that every season has a specific purpose and that we can't thrive without the other, we begin to see expectant hope for where we can potentially go.

It is with intent that I place harvest to blossom, blossom to harvest in this specific order. Harvest to blossom is that time in our life when we move from doing great things or intense efforts into rest and an off-season before starting up to repeat it again. Blossom to harvest is that time in our life when we begin to see the new beginnings, renewed hope that we will see abundance again and then see it through to full completion.

Harvest is joyful but also accompanied by labor—much labor. Harvest is measured and weighed with the intent of proving the outcome of the fruit. We fixate on harvest as the place we want to identify with as it is the point of achievement and measurement. We look and compare ourselves with others who we perceive to be producing as our standard and goal. It is rarely spoken that harvest is not always glamorous. Harvest can be very intense and requires great strength and stamina. It is a season that can't be sustained nonstop, day in and day out, year in and year out.

There must be a stopping point, a down season, so that the drive necessary to remain healthy during these abundant times will be sustained for future high seasons.

It is also important to understand that harvest is not our enemy: it is our goal and is of great importance. We must recognize the necessity and granted freedom to experience and embrace the so-called "off" seasons, which in all reality are very much "on" but not perceived as such. These seasons are of utmost importance to produce and be productive with our missions we embark upon with our life. Consider this: harvest is relatively short-lived, the end mark to what has been nurtured and prepared for in each and every other season. It is here that we recognize the great value of all the seasons, not just harvest.

It is with great sadness that many have been scorned for moving out of harvest into seasons of rest and care, as if the season of harvest never ends. This is crazy but true. Unrealistic expectations can leave one personally and outwardly wanting. Leaves fall and trees appear to be barren during this time, activity seems to be still and rightfully so as it is also with our lives. Fall has its glory with colorful images and tasting the satisfaction of the work that has been done; on the other hand, winter can seem lifeless in terms of outward appearances, when in reality much is happening on the inside.

Winter forces dormancy, a state of suspension where activity is devoid of external evidence. We tend to downplay its importance and underestimate rest and care. The amount of energy, strength, drive, and determination in high production must take this route of recovery and regrouping to be able to return to elevated levels of high output once again. Winter can be difficult emotionally as it can seemingly drag along. Many neglect to embrace it in stride. We must not throw away our confidence in seasons of dormancy, for it is here that plans and purposes are given and restored. We will all experience what may feel like a long winter. This is where embracing seasons gets very good. Your time will come to move out of dormancy and into a new path of activity: be patient and full of hope.

Buds turning to blossoms are the first sign of renewed life. When they appear, how sweet the smell and the sight. Blossoms are candy for the eyes and fragrance to the nose. When blossoms appear, you know that winter is over and seasons are changing. There are times when although in full blossom it may appear winter has returned, but this is short-lived, as seasons will continue to change. After coming through a long period of winter, sensing the beginning of blossoms is warmth to the soul. Stay focused on what you know is turning a corner: when blossoms are present, sunshine and warmth are on the way. It is here that the transition of seasons finds its place. Having moved from harvest to blossom takes in half of the growing process. Never neglect or place this set of seasons as invalid, for in doing so we simply become ineffective in our next round of harvest.

Once summer arrives, all that has been imagined becomes a reality. Life is at its full. It seems that all is moving forward at an accelerated speed. This is a wonderful yet vulnerable time as everything is in full motion. What seemed to take so long now begins to look a lot like that of full life again. Rolling back around to harvest is a critical time. If the details of rest, care, and preparation were not properly taken, harvest can and will be a breaking point. Due to neglect, many have taken great tolls when work is at its peak. There is a time to rest and a time to work with great determination. When it comes to rest, be sure to truly rest, not supplementing open space with additional activities that in turn may leave you tired and depleted. It is easy to fill seasons of rest with activities that take loads of energy and the purpose of rest is missed. When working the harvest, give it your all and see this season through to its full potential and completion. Seasons have purpose and in the light of hope and restoration, embrace and enjoy every step of the way through each one.

There is a time for everything, and a season for every activity under heaven.

(ECCLESIASTES 3:1)

CHAPTER 5

OBLIGATION

"Let your life be filled with what truly produces traction: true, full, and vibrant life. Let go of unnecessary and unhealthy obligations."

Troy

"It is not you; it is me." "At some point a line was crossed and what once brought life and joy has become obligation." These were the words spoken from my lips as I explained my resignation from my staff position. Twenty years of nondenominational church work as an associate pastor, youth director, music leader, and attending all planned meetings was very full. Alongside these responsibilities also required working outside of the church to support our family's financial needs. Through many of these years, eighty-hour workweeks were common as I worked bivocationally, with family time, exercise, and rest on top of this. This lifestyle was not the exception but the normal. Everyone has their story; this is not me being a "me monster" trying to outdo everyone else's story. Where was the voice of reason? Unfortunately, most organizations want every ounce of our being fully committed to their benefit and cause without recognition of boundaries that are healthy for all involved. I did not pay attention to the signs until a visit to the medical doctor revealed that there was nothing that could be done beside changing the way of life

I lived. In short, this meant backing off the intensity. I did not want to be "shipwrecked"; in my frame of mind, slowing down or not doing enough would be lacking importance and worse yet, viewed as weakness. This was a great misinterpretation of the meaning of shipwrecked, yet in so many ways we live as if we can never stop and regroup for fear of failure. I believe there are a great deal of people who can relate to this. That which started as life-giving becomes the premise for spiritual, emotional, and physical impoverishment due to too many overextensions. Good things become overbearing. It is here that Spun Out has its full definition.

Living life in overdrive can only be sustained for a limited amount of time. Living driven and overextended does not just apply to a vocation; it can also very much apply to all circumstances and situations that fill our personal lives. There is a ceiling to the use of energy and strength available to the user. This is a fairly simple concept to observe by the nature of most everything around us. Every living item has a life cycle and a need for refueling, maintenance, and recovery. Our output in all arenas of life have an expiration date affixed to them. This is not a negative when placed in context of the previous discussion of seasons, as there is a time to work and a time to rest.

The question then becomes, "What are the specifics in our lives that are no longer producing life, but rather are fulfilled out of draining obligation?"

Obligations to worthy commitments are not to be dropped and voided of responsibility simply because we want out of what we chose. There are many civil and personal responsibilities that we will engage in for a lifetime. By no means are we to bail out on precious commitments that we have devoted our life to. It is of great importance to look as deeply as possible into long-term decisions and choices before they are made. With this in mind, we can either adjust or remove certain activities and things that are no longer producing life-giving results. Typically, we hang on due to concluding that "we have to," when in all reality there are always options. What we commit to should produce life, joy, and peace; if it does not, take a closer look at what can be changed or rearranged.

When we owned nineteen sled dogs (exactly what we needed to make our life less full, ha ha), we were obligated to feed, run, and care for them each and every day. We made the commitment to the details of dogs, training dogs, and racing. In this we never failed to show up to meet their needs. There were early mornings, late evenings, and training runs that were not convenient. Nonetheless, the dedication and faithfulness to this discipline was fueled by healthy obligation we had chosen to engage in. Mushing for us had a season of over ten years, and then the time came when dialing it back and selling the main race team made the most reasonable sense. All those dogs brought an abundance of life and joy; I'm not so sure about peace, but it was a great ride while this season lasted. The decision of spending time with my wife and children along with time for others became a greater priority than spending hours with dogs each day. Was it hard to let go? Yes. Was it right? Yes. Did letting go and making a major change produce life? Absolutely. The point here is that we could have continued on, we could have continued winning races, but it would have been a drain and a negative obligation rather than one that produced life, joy, and peace.

It is in the context of being Spun Out that obligation takes on another question of "Why do we do what we do?" Do we function from a place of passion or a place of passivity? If what was at one time a passion is now rooted in obligation and is done more out of "I have to" rather than "I get to," there is reason for question. In whatever we do, if our answer is a "have to," then why do we continue to do it? Make adjustments, get refocused, remember the why, the reason, and let go of the heaviness. We are speaking here of obligations that at one time started as dreams, full of life, enthusiasm and passion. It is easy to forget where we started and the desires we had to engage in our current commitments. We can shift our passiveness back to passion. It will require making room for the purpose of "what we do" by coming back to "the why" we do it.

Commitments are a result of our decisions and choices. Understand there are circumstances that determine commitments, unmovable items that come into our lives that become obligations we did not plan for. It is

27

imperative that in these circumstances we keep our priorities set on those most important to us. We have activities we embrace that in all reality are not necessary. Variety can be a good thing, but too much exertion in too many activities and responsibilities leads to a run-down, overextended, overloaded way of life. It is wise to evaluate why we are engaged with the activities we have in our life. There are many good things that need to be placed on hold or completely taken out so that other areas of our life can have a higher priority. Letting go of attachments is not easy, as many times they are very good things in and of themselves, but when evaluations are made and decisions final, life begins to open up and breathe anew.

Evaluation of what we fill our life with and the obligations that accompany them is a large task. This is due to the question of what we should let go of and what we should hold on to. In some instances this is obvious, in others not so much. A proven guideline is to determine "Could I?" or "Should I?" There are many opportunities presented to us every day. Some come with minimum requirements, yet when compounded with several others they can become quite consuming. There are other choices that are in the long-term or lifetime category. These should require a closer view before we take the opportunity. Whether great or small, the question of "Could I?" is relevant. There are many things we can do, but the more important question is "Should I?" Is this really something that is for me, or does it simply sound good and make me feel important? We want to live in the space of what we *should* be doing.

Another test in this arena is to look at "the" versus an "a"/ "an" mentality. "The" mentality is very specific, "a" or "an" is quite general. The words of the greatest teacher of all time, Jesus, in the Bible, the book of John 14:6, put it thus: "I am *the* way, *the* truth and *the* life, no one comes to the father but through me." The word "the" is singular, signifying one way. To replace the word "the" with the word "a" completely changes the entire context and meaning of a foundational teaching of Christ. "*The*" was specifically chosen as the language of singularity. In the same way, we have many "the" and "a"/ "an" decisions and opportunities. For example: my wife, Linda, is "the" woman I have chosen to be committed to both by marriage vows and by daily life commitments. Other women who show interest in me and want to engage in a relationship are "an" option, but not "the" woman I am committed to. It keeps priorities clear when viewed through these eyes. So it is and applies to everything in our lives. Place the activity, name the thing: is it "a" way or is it "the" way?

There are two proven truths for determining this from a Christ follower perspective: First, what does the Word of God, the Bible, say as the directive? Second, what is the Holy Spirit that indwells believers in Jesus Christ guiding in this particular decision? If you do not know Christ personally, he is available and wants to partner with you (see "Knowing Christ" in the back of this book). It would be wrong to leave the impression that we do not analyze and use our God-given mind to observe and cross-examine the "the" versus an "a" decision. We need to use all of the resources we have to make correct choices. Combining the spiritual, mental and emotional with the physical is all important to coming to final conclusions.

One last thought before leaving obligation: when seeking direction, "No" can be and many times is more valuable than "Yes" as a directive. If we do not have the personal ability or someone in our life who can tell us "No" and respect it, we are far from being able to avoid unnecessary obligations. Healthy relationships allow us to make decisions both for or against commitments. There are no excuses for laziness and being unmotivated to do what we know is our responsibility. There is a time to communicate clearly that our life is at the full mark to those who are asking more from us. Trust in relationships is built upon clear understanding, not manipulation and control. It will be quite normal to say "No" often and "Yes" with reservation to avoid unnecessary obligations. When "Yes" is right, it will bring fulfillment and will be marked with traction, known as joy and peace.

It is for freedom that Christ has set us free. Stand firm, then, and do not let yourselves be burdened again by a yoke of slavery.

(GALATIANS 5:1)

STEP THREE

PACE

CHAPTER 6

86 MILES TO TOMBSTONE

"Setting pace in our life, circumstances, commitments, obligations, and choices will make us or break us. Making it is possible! We do not have to be broken and run-down!"

Troy

August 21, 1987, Nogales Mexico, Hwy 82 to Hwy 80, an 86-mile destination to Tombstone, Arizona. This was the third stage of seven in the Tour of the Future Road Cycling National Road Race for the best young riders of USA Cycling to compete and provide proving grounds for upcoming talented athletes. It was here that I crossed the finish line with hands raised high, with plenty of space from the chasing pack of riders to savor the victory of the day. It was on this day that a series of correct pacing decisions were made that ultimately brought home the win.

Pacing our life is much like pacing an athletic event. In the world of racing bicycles or running a dog sled race (pick your event), pace is everything! Go too slow and you are left behind, go too fast and you are left in burnout. Setting pace is an art. It requires fine attention to detail. When these details are given the proper place, it makes the entire experience much more enjoyable. There is nothing more frustrating, painful, and discouraging than bonking (an athlete's term for running out of fuel, more simply said, "I am done") and not making the intended finish line or objective. As much as I know victory, I have also known defeat. In the 2015 Mountain Bike Cross Country National Championships in Sun Valley, Idaho, on lap 2 of a 7-mile, 4,000 ft. climb, I hit the wall, in athletic terms blew up, done, finished, shut down and spun out (no spin of the pedals left). The reality of pushing too hard of a pace in the 22 miles of lap one became undeniable. I had overestimated my ability on the lower portion of this climb and ate a nutrition product I had not used before, causing a lack of breathing depth. I saw the finish line this day, but it was because I was forced to go back to it rather than through it—ouch!

Athletic events are by our choice. I have often asked myself, "Why do you do this, entering these events?" There is something wrong with us people who think suffering on purpose is a happy occurrence, yet there are others who continue to join me. Although we can compare life to an athletic event, the story and outcome of real life is not a sport, not a game that is put away or set aside. At one time I would have said, "Everything in life is easy compared to road racing bicycles"; now having lived some life, I would say, "Road racing bicycles is easy compared to living life." Happenings of life are very real, both by choice and otherwise.

Somehow, we tend to believe that we will personally be exempt from items like the law of gravity. The ground is hard, and solid items win when our physical body hits them. I learned this loud and clear the morning of Feb. 13, 2013, when I flipped my dog sled in a sharp corner and proceeded to hit a solid fence post with my right leg. The fence post won that day, and I broke rather than it. Oh, that fence post! Being positive is a great attribute and we should always believe for the best, but no mental strategy will stop the natural world we live in. We should have great faith for a safe and protected life, but also we should have great respect for that which is revolving around us. When "things" happen, the cry often is "Why, God?" when in all reality the question should be "What is in this?" Very simply, life happens and when it does, it is the greatest opportunity to embrace that God is there in life with us. True peace is not found in perfect circumstances, but rather in an ongoing relationship with Christ. Understanding this will stop the "why" questions and set us up to keep moving forward rather than stopped in the questioning of our circumstances.

Setting pace in our life, circumstances, commitments, obligations, and choices will make us or break us. Making it is possible! We do not have to be broken and run-down! Let's talk reality; run too hard, too far, and for too long the results will not change: they will end in being Spun Out. Another analogy from cycling is a condition referenced as being overspun. This occurs when speed is faster than the highest gear. Typically, this occurs on long descending grades where the ability to use gears to go faster is no longer available. The cadence of the legs is much too fast to maintain or have any productive use due to the gear being run out or overspun. To try to continue pushing forward like this is ineffective. We tend to stay in, "keep pushing forward," as the standard mode of operation. This is destructive to our form and our pace as it puts us into hyperfunction living, like a hummingbird on caffeine. Coffee in excessive amounts causes eyes to twitch, according to our local Starbucks barista (this is relative to each coffee connoisseur intake maximum). Likewise, our pace and demand in living can be beyond our spiritual, emotional, and physical maximum. Limits and boundaries in this context are not the enemy but rather exist for our benefit, not our disabling.

The other extreme is backing off when it is time to move forward. Pacing too slowly will place stress upon us and those around us. There is a sweet spot in momentum where the weight (load) is less due to forward progress. There is a physics formula according to Newton's Law that in modern terms would read: *the rate of change of momentum is proportional to the net force and is in the direction of that force.* Let it be with our pace that we allow the right amount of drive (force) to move us forward without lagging and causing unnecessary friction, frustration, or labor. It is easy to become unaware of our loss of momentum until we are placed within a trial. In terms of a time trial in cycling, we see if we are up to the standard pace. Do not become discouraged when under pressure, as it is in times of evaluation due to circumstances (trials) that we see our true north (accurate direction) and the pace of our life momentum revealed.

Pace has been a way of life for our family. We have started and maintained a sign and graphics business, ministered to youth and adults in multiple church settings, written and recorded music, raised children, and engaged in multiple sports activities. My wife, Linda, is a competitive sailor, cyclist, card player, and swimmer (note: competitive); Julia is a Homecoming Queen, an accomplished college student, and sled dog racer (raced at a professional level); Curtis a black belt in taekwondo, accomplished bass guitar player, and mountain bike racer (he knows how to knock you out); and for me, road, mountain, gravel bicycle racing, and sled dog racing to name a few. Having applied pacing highly to athletics, business, ministry, family, and the big picture of life, scores of hours have been spent learning the intricacies of setting and adjusting pace. This has produced many podium finishes for each one of us.

I have listed here some basic concepts and learning points to pace setting that can apply to any area of our life: 1. Start small and increase as you gradually build. 2. Build upon a foundation of knowledge—get information. 3. Set realistic goals; anything worth your time takes time. 4. Stay focused; avoid side trails. 5. Maintenance is always better before the breakdown; prevention rules over failure. 6. Sprint, mid distance and endurance are all related, but each requires its own discipline; define the what. 7. Add variety; overrepetition produces static results. 8. If it does not work, find solutions. 9. Stay within your known range; small overextensions create healthy stretching, large overextensions are demoralizing. 10. Fuel and refuel before thirst and hunger strike; when you're empty, you're empty. 11. Peak performance must be meticulously maintained to be sustained. 12. Know the condition you are in, not the condition you were at or wish for; proceed accordingly. 13. Learn from others but do not change who you are; this applies to whatever starting line you are on. 14. Save your greatest efforts for the right moments, live in the sweet spot, and soar when it is time to soar—think Eric Clapton on guitar or Lincoln Brewster. 15. Savor the victories and repeat.

Setting the correct pace in life is about finishing strong, not Spun Out on the sideline, maintaining a consistent level of output, remaining in the race, and recovering to keep driving forward. We all have a different course in life to fill and live. One does not supersede the other, whether you are fighting for a marriage, fighting for health, lonely because of the loss of a loved one, single, parent of children that are yours or adopted, a single parent, recovering from addiction, divorced, burned out, hard-driving entrepreneur, business professional, ministry leader, pursuing a career, college student, and the list goes on. Whatever defines you, it's your story, your life, your "unique to you" race. If you have been over-paced or underpaced, make corrections and adjustments. The purpose of pace is to alert us that we need to set pace as a life principle. Personally, if I had understood the application of pacing life earlier in our life journey, it would have saved time, unnecessary effort, and a whole lot of emotional energy. It is necessary to understand the value of pace in our professional, family, and personal life. Set a healthy pace and see the podium for you in every area of your life!

I press on toward the goal to win the prize for which God has called me heavenward in Christ Jesus.

(PHILIPPIANS 3:14)

CHAPTER 7

CADENCE CIRCLES

"What should be a completed cycle, when broken, produces a 'broken link' that creates symptoms in our well-being, spirit, soul, and in our physical body."

Troy

Circles, cylinders, and loops—they are part of our everyday experience. They apply to most everything around us in spiritual, emotional, and physical operation. Everything that is created functions on some order of cycle. Our galaxy is in circular motion, the earth rotates, daily sun rising and setting, seasons change, the big picture of a constant continuum of spherical motion. One of my favorite cycles due to its fascinating function is the circadian rhythm—ever heard of that? Circadian rhythm is any biological process that displays an endogenous (built-in, self-sustained), entrainable (adjustment to environment) oscillation of about 24 hours (cadence). These 24-hour rhythms are driven by a circadian clock (patterns of time), and they have been widely observed in plants, animals, and humans. Study further if it interests you, but for the purpose here, it is a fascinating ongoing circular, repeating, healthy, and necessary pattern.

There are many patterns that create ongoing circles in our own lives.

Some are short daily patterns that are part of our everyday living, and others engage days, months, years, and a lifetime. With this in mind, there are circumstances that bring about circles we will navigate through. These may be named as circumstances, journeys, experiences, situations, embarkments, trials, and challenges. When completed, satisfaction, balance, and general well-being are characterized as a result. If circles are not completed, the opposite effect will set in: frustration, discontentment, discouragement, a sense of failure, and an unhealthy state of being. What should be a completed cycle, when broken, produces a "broken link" that creates symptoms in our well-being both spirit (the real you), soul (mind will and emotions), and in our physical body.

"Broken links" cause healthy cycles to lose momentum as the connection for sustained drive is disconnected. Broken links will have effects upon us, until they finally become crippling or known or unknown cause for discouragement and frustration. It is guaranteed that at some point in our life cycles, we will experience circumstances causing difficulties, hurts or discouragements that can be ambiguous to explain or pinpoint. And then in many cases the root cause is very obvious and needs no deep searching. Rather than ignoring the issues, we need to recognize broken links for what they are and pinpoint the damaged broken link in us. It is not a matter of overanalyzing every detail of our life, but rather recognizing that there may be a specific reason for struggling though a difficulty in our life. When we recognize a specific point of brokenness, it allows us to deal with the cause. When we know the cause, we can then start upon a road of healing and reconnecting the link that was broken. This requires strong character, humility, making wrongs right, forgiveness, communication, restructuring, accepting responsibility, and a purposeful desire to repair and move on.

Healing has degrees; some wounds are surface level and can be dealt with swiftly while getting back on track is sure. Other wounds are deep and require extensive time to repair. I can relate to this on the physical level after breaking my right leg two separate times. We can all relate to physical wounds and challenging bodily conditions that have been through a healing process and resolved. There are also conditions that we live with that need resolve. This also heavily applies to our soul. Our soul makes up our mind, will, and emotions, and takes continual hits from situations and circumstances around us each day. It is vitally important to guard our mind and emotions, for it is here the most damaging broken links take place. Spiritually, humanity has a broken heart, separated from God, lost, and searching for the connection to what will repair the link of spiritual despair. Humanity has looked far and wide for spiritual answers and the answer lies fully in God, specifically in knowing Jesus Christ as Lord personally. He is the answer to the spiritual broken link. (See "Finding Christ" at the back of this book.)

Cadence applies to a rhythmic sequence of motion or activity. Much like the speed of pedal strokes when riding a bicycle, we set our lives on a certain tempo of cadence. Our life cadence is adjusted by the decisions and choices we make. We do have the ability to determine what cadence we will set for our life. Wind life up too much and it involves over-spinning. We often reference this as being overloaded, overextended, or Spun Out. The rhythm we set and the cadence we keep is the difference between sustainable life or burnout. It is of utmost importance to recognize the cadence tempo we are on; are we running crazy in circles, or completing a circle that has significance, satisfaction, and purpose? If the spin of our life is over the top, it can only be held for a limited amount of time. When overspun, our form in general becomes sloppy and we tend to not do our best at any one task. Relate this to riding a bicycle and the pedals are spinning so fast you cannot keep up with their speed. This does not look or feel right. It is here that many great men and women have taken a fall or compromised; too much, too fast without boundaries controlling the overwhelming pace of life. Cadence is not only worth serious planning and consideration but should also be continually evaluated as a way of life.

In our life, circles of tasks, healing, projects, relationships, building, entrepreneurship, education, personal growth, and others will have different levels of time commitments, both short, in-between, and long cycles. Some we will strive to complete with the end in sight and others are an ongoing continuum with the end result far in the distance. Coming full circle has four distinct steps throughout the start-to-finish process. Think in terms of a circle within a square. Each of the points of the square have a purpose in the process. Progress can be identified with each of the four points when reached moving around the circumference of the circle.

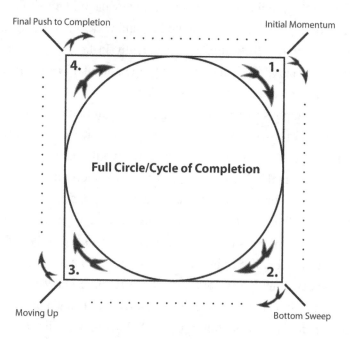

First, the top front corner in motion moving downward clockwise. The beginning of any cycle has momentum, whether it be a positive endeavor or viewed as a difficult circumstance. This is the point where gravity, physical or nonmaterial, has its greatest pull. Getting started is typically the most enthusiastic, strong and positive. It is easy to get excited about new endeavors. We must always keep at the forefront of our thinking, the commitment that we are embarking upon. Starting in some cases requires an incredible deal of effort to get moving. It is of great importance to realize there will be required energy that must be sustained to keep what was started alive and in motion. Endeavors are relatively easy to start, sometimes much too easy; it takes dedication and renewed commitment to take it full circle. As we walk through life, some of these cycles happen not by choice, but are rather forced upon us. These are the cycles in our lives that come upon us by surprise. Of all the circumstances in our life, the ones we do not choose can be the most challenging, as their starting momentum can be at a staggering accelerated pace.

Second, from the bottom corner sweeping across to the adjacent bottom corner of the square points in the circle. It is the one we reference as the bottom. After the initial momentum has taken place and much has been accomplished (a great deal of energy, time and resources have been used), reality and realization sets in for the need to pull harder in the fight to keep what was started in motion. This motion is no longer pushing down with gravity, but rather pulling backward. It is a life-changing moment when we realize that completing a cycle is not all about driving momentum forward. Sweeping the bottom can come swift and unexpected. This is the place where giving up, giving in, feeling trapped, and loss of momentum begin to set in, simply stated, "bottomed out." Sweeping across the bottom requires traction, and that traction is knowing it is part of the cycle—we do not stay here.

Third, moving from the bottom corner up to the top back corner. Here lies the motion of lifting and moving up. Lifting is a power stroke. Moving up is encouraging no matter the pace. There is something great to be experienced knowing we are on the upstroke. Lifting takes effort, but it is also accompanied by the knowledge that momentum has shifted and is taking us up. Sweeping across the bottom was necessary to build speed and desire for this phase of completing the circle. Coming up brings renewed vision. It is here that we begin to remember why we started what we did in the first place. It is also here that we gain glimpses of hope that we will not be held in the same circumstances or situation we have been working through. As challenging as lifting is, whatever it is that you are pushing through, enjoy this portion of the process as glimpses of completion began to come into sight.

Fourth, completing the circle from the back, top point to the front, forward beginning point. This is bringing the whole process around to completion. There is a distinct knowing when something is finished or fully completed. Pushing across the top has its own share of effort, as completing a circle is not fully accomplished until the final details are set in place. We need to make it a goal and top priority to see what we start through to completion. Don't be caught coming up short at the close of a full circle. As cycles close, the choice then is given as to whether we repeat, renew the process, or leave the endeavor alone.

For those circles that we often repeat, we can learn how to be more efficient in the next cycle. It is when cycles are repeated time and time again with efficiency and excellence that great accomplishments are accompanied with a sweet cadence. Cadence is related to momentum; once it is in motion, it is a powerful means of forward motion. When cadence is set to high, the condition of being Spun Out creeps up on us. Setting our cadence, which relates to pace, is a fine line, but must be prioritized and analyzed to keep from crossing the line of too much. In our relationships, families, business, churches, athletics, education, and personal life, we should prioritize finishing circles of importance, repair broken links that hinder or stop progress, and set our sights on rounding out cadence cycles to full completion.

In the heavens he has pitched a tent for the sun....
  It rises at one end of the heavens and makes its circuit to the other; nothing is hidden from its heat.

                                                        (PSALM 19:4–6)

CHAPTER 8

GOLDEN CHARLIE

"Hope restores our endurance, restored endurance fuels hope, and the result of the two working together builds strong faith that will take us over into completion and a full cycle."

Troy

As the sun was setting, zero-degree temperatures gave way to warm pink and fire-red Idaho winter skies. Pieces of finely crafted ash dog sled lay splintered around the base of a solid 6-inch round fence post, the only object available to stop the unstoppable train of ten sled dogs. One missed trail command led to a frozen creek offshoot, leaving musher and dog sled on one side of a barbed wire fence and ten wound-up race dogs that had gone through the fence pair by pair on the other side. This was a treacherous situation, as the only possible way to get corrected was to bring the dogs and lines back through the fence heading in the correct direction. To accomplish this task took several hours of navigating barbed wire, tangled lines, frustrated dogs, freezing cold, wet feet, and darkness. To make matters more interesting, it was Thanksgiving and this was to be a short 8-mile evening dog run before the turkey would be taken out of the oven.

It was in this moment that I really got to know Charlie, a large golden

Alaskan husky that ran in the wheel position (just ahead of the sled) due to his incredible drive, focus, and strength. Charlie was a new addition to our dog sled team this particular winter season, and in the rearrangement and switching around of every dog getting back through the fence, my main leaders, Tempest and Prancer, ended up in the back and Charlie in the front. The entire team was confused and frustrated with the waiting, but one dog stood tall and with confidence, strength, and a level head, led the team back home. It was from this happening we discovered Charlie was the leader of leaders. He became our winning success and left a legacy of intuition, drive, and endurance to our dog kennel.

Healthy endurance is not only about enduring long: it is knowing how to apply pace over the course of distance. To be successful in life, we will be characterized by endurance which is made up of patience, perseverance, and the ability to withstand hardship and adversity. We all need some Charlie in us. When all seems to go long, wrong, upside down and sideways, we keep our head up, we lead, we don't lay down, we stand up and press on.

One of the most inspiring accounts of endurance is that of Ernest Shackleton's *Endurance* voyage. The year was August 1914, in England, when Captain Ernest Shackleton and twenty-seven crewmen set sail for Antarctica aboard the ship *Endurance,* where he planned to cross the last uncharted continent by foot. In January 1915 after battling its way through a thousand miles of pack ice and only a day's sail short of its destination, *Endurance* became locked in an island of ice. For ten months the ice drifted northwest before the ship was finally crushed between two ice floes and sank. With no options left, Shackleton attempted a near-impossible journey over 850 miles of the South Atlantic's heaviest seas. Their survival and the survival of the men they left behind depended upon their small lifeboat successfully finding the island of South Georgia, a tiny dot of land in a vast and hostile ocean. Ernest Shackleton unbelievably made it to South Georgia Island. He returned with a rescue craft four-and-a-half months later to the crew left behind on Elephant Island in the Drake Passage, South Atlantic Ocean, and all crew members survived and returned to England. A story of great perseverance and amazing endurance. Shackleton had a great deal of Charlie attitude in him.

Hope is vital to healthy endurance, as it sets a mark as to what is the desired end. There are many circumstances and situations that can appear hopeless. We have two options: lay down, allow fear and defeat to grip us or rise up in boldness and fight forward. Hope is an essential component to healthy endurance and is foundational at its core. It was hope that drove the *Endurance* expedition and Ernest Shackleton to continue pressing on when all appeared to be an unattainable task. If Shackleton had given in and stopped attempting to further the plan of survival, the amazing story told above would not exist. Did it appear hopeless? Absolutely yes, but in the midst of the trial, hope was continually renewed. It was the same with Charlie and me: we had an unwavering hope that we would complete the daunting task of getting untangled, back through the barbed wire and off the frozen stream, making it home to a bowl of dog food and meat snack for Charlie and a soft warm bed and a cooked Thanksgiving turkey dinner for me, hopefully not overcooked!

Endurance requires purpose, reason, commitment, motive, an undying and unwavering desire to continue to fight all the way to the finish. It is in the expectation of what lies at the finish and in the end result that our hope is built, rekindled, and sustained. The challenge lies in overcoming the enemies of endurance: we must have answers to overcome them. For example, here are five enemies to endurance and answers that overcome and create continued perseverance: enemy number one: I want to quit. Answer: If I quit now, all that has been gained will be lost. What I have done has value—don't stop now. Number two: This is hard. Answer: Anything worth investing in is not easy; over time the struggle will only produce more strength. I am getting stronger (the stronger the wind, the stronger the trees!). Number three: Stuck and in a rut. Answer: Keep moving, outsmart the challenge. Much is learned and accomplished in times of difficulty. I will press on and keep all options open, no matter how I feel. Number four: Progress is slow. Answer: Slow progress is more progress than no progress. Keep moving and keep it alive. Number five: The fuel level is empty. Answer: Refuel often and have a plan as to when. Energy will be lost: put in the necessary recovery ingredients and recharge.

Endurance is embracing the ongoing feat of whatever comes our way, whether we chose or did not choose the task at hand. In 2003, my wife and I took over a small sign and graphics company that was less than six months old. We truly believed then and still believe today that this business was a gift and a surprise from God. Essentially it was a startup company with a skeleton of equipment and supplies. Today, years later, Windy City Arts, Signs and Graphics is the premier sign company in the renowned Sun Valley, Idaho. Business has been rewarding and also taxing. Many people, us alike, ask for and long for blessing or desire prosperity, but do not fully understand in the asking what this means. It means a great deal of hard work, personal expansion, extended effort, long days and nights, emotional energy, physical energy, planning, organizing, and unexpected challenges. Our business has brought great reward and the rewards outweigh the challenges, but with that said, there have been many seasons of simply putting our posture forward, spirit, soul and body, and pushing through some difficult business navigation. We would not be where we are today without applying principles of endurance each day, month, and year that have gone by.

Endurance is made up of perseverance and patience. It is in the process of endurance that development in our life fully takes place. We grow deeper and more established as we continually point at our desired end results, the goal, product, or produce. That which is produced in or through our life can be that of internal or external value. This is where our hope becomes vital to our carrying out those things we have committed to or engaged with that require an ongoing pursuit. It is in hope that we can endure the current situations we are in and going through, because we can look to the desired finish line or completion. Hope produces joy, confidence, and peace that can come only through expectation; without it, despair sets in. We tend to want things to be resolved as quickly as possible, and this is where patience needs to take a front seat in our enduring.

The longer we endure and persevere, the greater our expectation will become.

Hope restores our endurance, restored endurance fuels hope, and the result of the two working together builds strong faith that will take us over into completion and a full cycle. Listed below is a flowchart of how hope gravitates to the fullness of faith and completion.

Hope (divine expectation) develops endurance/perseverance/ patience in the waiting.

But if we hope for what we do not yet have, we wait for it patiently.

(ROMANS 8:25)

Hope is the predecessor to faith.

Now faith is being sure of what we hope for and certain of what we do not see.

(HEBREWS 11:1)

Faith is the product of what is hoped for.

Now faith is being sure of what we hope for and certain of what we do not see.

(HEBREWS 11:1)

It is faith that pleases God.

But the man who has doubts is condemned if he eats, because his eating is not from faith; and everything that does not come from faith is sin.

(ROMANS 14: 23)

Embrace hope leading to faith, and let endurance/perseverance/patience work!

This process is always backed up by the power of the Holy Spirit.

May the God of hope fill you with all joy and peace as you trust in him, so that you may overflow with hope by the power of the Holy Spirit.

(Romans 15:13)

The produce or the product of endurance/perseverance/patience is continually growing inside of us and should be marked by hope (divine expectation) and joyful expectancy.

But if we hope for what we do not yet have, we wait for it patiently.

(Romans 8: 25)

The longer we wait, work out the product, the greater the development of the produce. We want it complete—this is what James was saying in James 1:4.

Perseverance must finish its work so that you may be mature and complete, not lacking anything.

(James 1:4)

STEP FOUR

BALANCE

CHAPTER 9

THAT ROCK

"Many have been caught up in the glory of fast-pace growth, only to find themselves out of balance and swept away from everything they held dear to their heart."

Troy

At the north beginning of the Book Cliff Range in Southeastern Utah, 1,500 feet above the small town of Helper, stands an iconic landmark, Balanced Rock. It is here on the towering cliffs Balanced Rock stands alone with sandstone cut out from around its base to make it an object of awe and wonder. The mystery as to how this stand-alone-in-the-sky rock feature continues to remain in place has captivated onlookers for hundreds of years. At the base of the rock it is narrow, and the top is a large square shape, making it appear precariously subject to falling at any given moment in time. Though wind, rain, storms, earthquakes and every natural enemy that has been thrown at it, the rock has remained in place. It is in and around this point that each morning of my childhood I would wake up, look out our front window to observe if "that rock" was still towering above our small town. To this day Balanced Rock stands solid and proud, demonstrating accurate proportions, stability, enduring strength, perseverance, and, most of all, a symbol of constant balance.

53

Balance is at the core of living life within the proper range that keeps us from becoming Spun Out. It is when we allow our life to become overrun, overwhelmed, overextended, overworked, overaggressive, overcapacity, overcommitted, overcrowded, overintense, overzealous, and many other "overs" that we find our living out of balance. As I looked to *Webster's Dictionary* for a few "over" words, I found that the list goes on and on: matter of fact, there are 1,681 references to words starting with "over." This is *over* the top! Addressing the issues of over-age in our personal life, family life, church life, business life, athletic life, recreation life, pet life (okay, we had nineteen dogs in the kennel at one time, so I am taking my own advice here), social media life, and all the things infiltrating us require our full attention and need to be sorted out. The greatest challenge is: where do we start in consideration of so much? We do not realize the volume we carry until we start analyzing how many activities we engage in on a regular basis.

Within the context of balance is a deeper quality of capacity. Looking around us—from God-made natural wonders to manmade inventions—we observe there is a limit to everything. Each and every being, be it living, mechanical, structural, emotional, natural, and spiritual, has certain boundaries and capacities. For example, a Formula One race car has an elite high-performance engine that functions under incredible RPM (between 15,000 and 20,000 possible), creating high horsepower and giving incredible speed. Within this scope are limited hours and capacities set by friction, heat, and wear. Each engine, though highly tuned, has a limiter that does not allow the RPM to exceed the maximum set for safe operation of the engine. Where this limiter is set determines a boundary so that the engine stays out of the danger zone and remains within safe operation. Limitations set boundaries on what otherwise would be unsafe or damaging outcomes.

We are all functioning with a certain capacity. There is a limit to our reservoir before we hit the overflow mark and everything downstream catches the excess. It is when we get outside of our range of appropriate operation that we become overwhelmed and begin to feel the burn of

Spun Out. Staying within a balanced range of limits is not only advisable but also essential to making it through each of life's cadence cycles. One of the most important aspects of balance is being able to say no. There will be many opportunities to say yes and then regret the commitment, as it does not produce life but rather a further unhealthy obligation. Evaluating opportunities is worth the time and effort as it can be the difference between a full life and a drained life. We have been asked if we are minimalists (one who is ultrarestrictive) due to suggesting that there is a time to say no, but rather we are opportunists looking for the right opportunity. We live in a culture of many offerings, all things begging for our attention and resources with the tag of "if you don't have this," you are somehow not complete or not in the current loop. I am not suggesting to be naïve, but rather selective as to what fills your life.

We have learned that in a complex world, the more we can simplify, the more room there is to excel at the matters that are most important. Applied to our business, we have taken what was spoken of and thought to be very complex and stripped away the unnecessary to make a simple process and superior product. In a church or organization setting, taking away the unnecessary and asking "Why do we do this?" and "What is its value?" allowed for simplicity to be the goal, breathing new life into the stagnated status quo. This is a good place to start asking questions and evaluating why and what are we committed to. There are many activities and commitments that are not wrong within themselves, but they are time, energy, and emotional thieves. We only have so much in our life account: make too many withdrawals and we become bankrupt. Make a list of the things that are of most importance. Placing items such as God, family, work (business), hobbies, and recreation in an order of importance and not wavering from it is extremely beneficial. Most of the urgent items presented to us as "really" important are not as essential and critical as we may be led to think.

Living a balanced life starts with a solid foundation. What may appear to be top-heavy and not falling over with every pressure has a substantial underworking of accurate proportions supporting the visible.

Take the roots of a tree, where it is often said that a tree is twice as big underground as it is above ground. The tree trunk, branches, and leaves we see are balanced and supported by an underlying network of stability. From a leadership perspective, it is unfair and unjust to continually add to an individual simply because they are available or appear to be capable of handling a task. A good leader investigates the strength of that foundation before adding weight that may not be sustained. Balance is the responsibility of both the initiator and the one committing to the task. We never want to be guilty of seeking a "yes" answer or giving a "yes" response only for our benefit. What is in the best interest of all involved should be at the forefront of every relationship, not what is the most beneficial to one party. This requires honesty and a commitment to the greater good of all involved.

Balanced foundations produce enduring strength and perseverance. We must continue to fortify the foundation, growing deeper to sustain what is visible. In the world of business, ministry, personal pursuits, and life endeavors, we often hear of failings due to "It simply got too big," or "It became out of control" or "It was more than I could handle." The more added, the more top-heavy our life will become, and it is inevitable that if the foundation being built upon is not adequate, there will be a breaking point. Foundations are infrastructure of the heart, soul, and physical body, personally speaking. Speaking of an organization or a business, the same principles apply, but the focus is applied to proper leadership and strategic expansion. Growth and being added to are typically noted as being very positive, and they very well are markers of forward progress, but not to be confused with thought-out planned growth and expansion. This applies fully across the board with all of life. When expansion happens quickly, the means to sustain it are of necessity. Many have been caught up in the glory of fast-paced growth, only to find themselves out of balance and swept away from everything they held dear to their heart. We must determine to have balance as a standard of our life. Add what is a right "yes" and take away what is an out-of-bounds "no."

As human beings, we are made up of three distinct parts—spirit, soul, and body. If we are out of balance in any of these specific areas, our life becomes inconsistent and unhealthy. In light of our engineering technological age, with great advancements and a continually changing set of information to digest, it is easy to become focused on items of the latest function and forget to care for our personal well-being. How do we balance our personal life?

First, keep the spirit healthy and alive. Your spirit is the real you, the one looking out on life from the inside. Our spirit is that which is made alive to God through Christ or separated from God if the choice is made to reject belief in God. Keeping a healthy daily input of spiritual life is vital to our spiritual being. Practice reading the Bible (the Word), prayer, worship, and walking with the guidance of the Holy Spirit.

Second, the soul. The soul is made up of our mind, will, and emotions. There cannot be enough said for keeping our thinking and mental state healthy. Our mind and emotions can become extremely overloaded, causing our will to be weak and susceptible to all kinds of bombardments. Think on the right things and weed out wrong thoughts and emotions. It requires self-control to keep the soul healthy. Much of this book in previous chapters ultimately has to do with our emotions; this is where many find themselves Spun Out with overload and overextensions. We need to fill our minds with the right perspectives to engage in hope and healthy thinking. Again, feed on the Word of God and good input. We live in a day and age where access to good teaching, reading, music, and Godly recourses has never been better. Always answer negative and wrong thoughts with words; God's Word always trumps any mental or emotional play.

Third, the physical body. Many books have been written as to how to care for our body. Everything from nutrition, proper exercise, getting enough sleep, and everything in-between. My purpose here is not to tell you what to do, because what works for me may be far from what works for you, but the point is: take care of yourself. You can only accomplish what you need to accomplish and be content to the degree that your physical body can function. We all have certain physical limitations; we need make the best of what we do have and place priority on staying healthy.

> *May God himself, the God of peace, sanctify you through and through. May your whole spirit, soul and body be kept blameless at the coming of our Lord Jesus Christ.*
>
> (1 Thessalonians 5:23)

STEP FIVE

ENCOURAGEMENT

CHAPTER 10

SHORE TO SHORE

"The root of hope is encouragement. Expectation comes when encouragement is given the opportunity to grow in the heart and soul of an individual, creating the right spark of motivation."

Troy

Encouragement has a profound effect upon those who receive it and to those who give it. To encourage, build up, strengthen, and support an individual or organization has become the sole purpose of our lives. It has been a Larsen family motto for Linda and me to pass down to our children that "we are here to be a blessing (encouragement) to others." If a day goes by without lifting someone up, or supporting them in a meaningful way, the day does not carry the same weight and significance. It is true that we need to encourage ourselves and rightfully so, but giving hope and purpose to others creates a fullness that does not come any other way. When we give, there is a receiving back that brings fulfillment and great satisfaction. When feeling discouraged, a good starting point to improve our emotion is to take the direction of encouraging someone else. Rather than staying focused on the condition we are in, look toward what you can say or do to lift up another. No matter how difficult our circumstance or situation, there is always someone else in need and guaranteed to be someone in greater discouragement and discontentment than our own.

The root of hope is encouragement. Expectation comes when encouragement is given the opportunity to grow in the heart and soul of an individual, creating the right spark of motivation. We should continually search to encourage and be encouraged, a reciprocating back-and-forth lifestyle of giving and receiving. Think of encouragement as being like the waves on the sea: they move continually from shore to shore. Be intentional about building others up and equally so toward our own need to find strength in hope. Some will play down the need of encouragement and put on a face of self-reliance, only to find that all is playing out well and then ... there is the "and then...." We should be strong and self-reliant, not continually looking to people to pick us up, but this reliance is not upon our own ability but rather a greater ability in us—this is the God factor that is available to us. (See "Finding Christ" at the back of this book.)

Through the years we have organized summer camps for junior high and high school students (part of twenty years of student ministry). One particular year we chose to host our camp in the mountains of Southeastern Utah. Planning the camp to fit our schedule landed us in mid-June. Depending upon where you live geographically, June is summer, a warm month. Our camp was chosen to be at a clear, tranquil, high mountain lake with wildflowers blooming all around us, perfect for visual aesthetics of the earth's beauty and God's creation. The important detail here is *high mountain*—9,000 feet elevation to be exact—which translates to night temperatures in the thirties and daytime highs in the comfortable seventies. At this time of year, we still had enough pockets of unmelted snow to have snowball fights at our "summer camp," and to make swimming comfortable, there was still ice floating in the lake from the spring thaw that was not quite complete.

The lake water was extremely cold and upon sunset one evening, we could hear a desperate cry for help coming across the water. We identified a small fishing boat with a single man overboard struggling in the water. Taking one of our camp canoes and several willing bright-eyed boys ready for adventure, we set out on a rescue mission. Upon our arrival, the man was in a great state of shock, and hypothermia had begun to set in. We began to look for options to get him back into his boat, but his muscles had locked up and shut down; as well, he was a very large man. We decided our only option was to connect a rope to his boat with our canoe, encourage him to hold on, and paddle hard, pulling him to the nearest shore. Here is where the going got tough: he was glad we were there, but all sense of hope had been lost from his perspective. He asked us to leave him and let him die; "I just can't hold on any longer." We encouraged him adamantly to stay with us. Part of the way to shore, he completely gave up both physically and mentally and let go of the back of his boat, to which one of us got into his boat, took his arms, and held him, dragging behind and encouraging him that we would be to shore soon. Upon reaching land he could not move, could not crawl, could not speak, but he could blink his eyes with gratitude that his life had not ended in that icy water grave. We helped load him (more like drag him) into his truck, and his wife took him away for medical attention. We all learned a deep level of encouragement that night, both for the man and for all of us doing everything we could to save his life.

Encouragement makes a world of difference in extreme situations. Even when the ones we are encouraging are giving up, our words, actions, and presence are the catalyst between life and death. Death can occur not only to our physical bodies, but also to our emotions and heart's desire. Having someone come alongside us in times of great need, to encourage and bring hope, is valuable but also a scarce occurrence. This should not be the case, but unfortunately it is easy to focus on our own survival and forget the needs of others. When glory is taken in someone else's failure and fall, something is quite wrong with this thinking as it is self-serving and full of pride. We see this mentality all around us, and so much more we must engage in encouraging and building others up. Encouragement and hope are precious and as with anything of value, they are not easily found in many of our surroundings, yet the access to them is not closed for a select few but rather available and waiting for those who choose to hold on, stay engaged, and take courage.

Found at the core of encouragement is courage. Courage is strength to carry on in spite of those things that come against us. There are many enemies to courage, fear being at the core fighting against us. We could make a long list of items that discourage us, but it all boils down to fear being at the core. My Grandpa and Grandma Larsen used to make maple syrup, 40 gallons of maple tree sap boiled down to make one gallon of syrup. For the most part fear and the reality of those fears are at about the same ratio, 40 to 1. Listed here are a few synonyms of fear: alarm, anxiety, dread, fearfulness, fright, horror, panic, scare, terror, trepidation, bother, worry, fret, fuss, stew, stress, sweat, trouble, agonize, chafe, despair. Fear is the direct enemy and it attacks our own and others' encouragement, hope, and faith. To take courage requires us to deal with fear directly. Fear has a way of making details that exist worse and bringing up details that don't exist as if they did. Fear is overcome by great courage. This is why when Jesus spoke the words, "Take heart, I have overcome the world"; early believers in Christ had every reason to be filled with fear as He was life-giving, yet those against Him wanted not only to destroy Him but all of his followers. Jesus' words gave early believers in Him courage with his words. These words also give us great hope because as we have Him with us, we are not limited to our current surroundings—we overcome. Fear is fought and conquered with words! This is why encouragement when spoken to ourselves and to others is so powerful and necessary to build courage against the challenges of life.

Speaking the right words in a given moment is of the essence. Taking a moment and allowing the right encouragement to be given will pay large dividends for the one being spoken to. There is nothing more demeaning than speaking harsh, critical, or embarrassing words to an individual and justifying it as an encouraging word. Knowing what words, how to speak them, and when is key to building one up. This is situational and requires reading into the moment. There have been times that calling out with a deep command was just the right method to get momentum moving in the right direction, and others where a soft whisper of gentleness was the correct touch to gain confidence. There is not a formula to encouragement, but rather being intentional about it. It helps to say to the one you are speaking to, "I would like to encourage you," and then do it. Make sure the message being given is truly uplifting and not taking the situation backwards. Also, along these lines, keep the message short and concise. Talking simply to talk is not going to encourage anyone. Say your planned words, bring hope, have healthy conversation about the encouragement, and be finished. Encouragement is not the final solution but rather a piece of something solid to hold on to in the moment of despair.

Negativity and negative words should not be a part of us. It has been said by psychologists that it takes seven positive comments to overcome one negative comment spoken. Honestly, by observation I believe that is on the optimistic side, which we should be on, but it takes constant positive reinforcement to overcome negative words and actions. Negativity destroys self-esteem, confidence, friendships, marriages, children, businesses, churches, leadership, organizations, and relationships on every level. We have watched particularly in our business and churches that when negativity infiltrates the ranks, the atmosphere for productivity and forward progress drops drastically. We do not allow it where we have the authority! Qualified leadership does not sanction negativity or engage in it. Although many so-called leaders practice this, it is the beginning of the end if not corrected. The reason being: trust is broken. Trust is the foundation in all relationships. Positions and jobs have been lost due to complaining, murmuring, sarcasm, unruly comments, and self-promotion. When one speaks negatively both towards others and an organization, it is a sure sign of their own lack of confidence and low valuation of self. Degrading others in any form is a means of building up and justifying an individual's self-pride. Those in authority using their position to downgrade or discredit others need to realize that authority is not given to abuse but rather to build up and encourage those under them.

We need to make corrections where necessary, ask for forgiveness, and make every effort to be on the side of encouragement.

Staying encouraged can be a constant everyday challenge for many. There is a difference between expectation, hope, faith, and excitement. We can be excited about certain aspects of our lives, but some circumstances and situations do not breed excitement, rather require deep commitment, to which we can remain encouraged to press on. This is the message of the cross that Jesus hung on for us, that He took our place so that we can be set free and press on (see "Finding Christ" at the end of this book). For those who appear to have a smooth life with everything going perfectly in their favor: if the truth be known, the need for encouragement due to hurts and pain exist and are a real daily occurrence. As the human race, there is not one of us exempt from needing hope in our times of need.

Be encouraged: you are not alone and there is nothing wrong with you for needing and looking for encouragement. If you have been "*Spun Out*," today is your day to get traction, see new hope, gain new expectation, and be encouraged.

For everything that was written in the past was written to teach us, so that through endurance and the encouragement of the Scriptures we might have hope.

(ROMANS 15:4)

EPILOGUE

My purpose is that they may be encouraged in heart and united in love, so that they may have the full riches of complete under-standing, in order that they may know the mystery of God, namely, Christ, in whom are hidden all the treasures of wisdom and knowledge.

(COLOSSIANS 2:2–3)

The purpose of this writing is that you will be encouraged to find **restored hope** and **healthy endurance**. Having walked through seasons of life that had brought what I thought to be shipwrecks, the realization that I was not broken but rather *dry-docked* in a place of restoration and care brought great encouragement. It is my desire that whatever season or circle of life that has brought you to Spun Out, you as well will be filled with the same divine expectation and endurance to continue moving forward. If you have been encouraged in any way that you are not broken, grounded, or in a hopeless standstill, these words have succeeded. Be encouraged!

Five Crucial Steps to Restored Hope and Healthy Endurance

Rest - Take time to recover and renew for your next endeavor.

Evaluation - Be realistic with what state your life is in. Is it time for *dry dock* or full sailing ahead?

Pace – It is your race. The tempo we set determines our endurance.

Balance - Let go of and add what rightfully belongs in your life.

Encouragement – Stay surrounded with the right people and words that lift you up.

KNOWING CHRIST

The greatest hope and encouragement we can ever obtain is found in personally knowing Jesus Christ. Listed below are Bible references that will lead you to knowing Christ.

For God so loved the world that he gave his one and only Son, that whoever believes in him shall not perish but have eternal life.

(JOHN 3:16)

For all have sinned and fall short of the glory of God, and are justified freely by his grace through the redemption that came by Christ Jesus.

(ROMANS 3:23–24)

For the wages of death, but the gift of God is eternal life in Christ Jesus our Lord.

(ROMANS 6:23)

That if you confess with your mouth, "Jesus is Lord," and believe in your heart that God raised him from the dead, you will be saved. For it is with your heart that you believe and are justified, and it is with your mouth that you confess and are saved.

(ROMANS 10:9–10)

For what I received I passed on to you as of first importance: that Christ died for our sins according to the Scriptures, that he was buried, that he was raised on the third day according to the Scriptures,

(1 CORINTHIANS 15:3–4)

For it is by grace you have been saved, through faith—and this not from yourselves, it is the gift of God—not by works, so that no one can boast. For we are God's workmanship, created in Christ Jesus to do good works, which God prepared in advance for us to do.

(EPHESIANS 2:8–10)

Therefore, if anyone is in Christ, he is a new creation; the old has gone, the new has come!

(2 CORINTHIANS 5:17)

Prayer to Knowing Christ: I ask you, Jesus, to be the Lord, the ultimate ruler of my life. Take all of me: I give my life to you. Jesus, I say that you came for me, died for me, and rose again to purchase God-given life for me. I choose to live each and every day from this day forward as a follower of Christ Jesus.

If you have given your life to Christ, or the contents of this book have encouraged you, we would love to hear your story. Send us an email at troydlarsenbooks@gmail.com.

CPSIA information can be obtained
at www.ICGtesting.com
Printed in the USA
LVHW101133170419
614497LV00006B/7/P